Lefties Unite!

This is your Cursive Writing Workbook

Name
_____

Some handy hints for helping your left-hander

Left-handers are 10% of the population and although neat handwriting can be a challenge, it is not impossible to achieve!

Left-handers can have problems with smudging and correct pen/pencil grip, posture, placement, and letter formation.

Here are some practical tips to assist the left-hander in your life to improve their handwriting skills:

* Buy equipment and resources made especially for left-handers.
* Encourage them to keep the page steady with their right hand while writing.
* Tilt the top of the page to the right parallel with the forearm, so they can see the tip of the pencil/pen.
* Make sure the left-hander has enough space when writing to avoid others bumping them.
* Because left-handers push the pen/pencil along the paper rather than pushing, by using a softer pencil it can help prevent smudging.
* Encouraging the use of right to left strokes on the crossbar lettering, (example t) can help.

These steps will help the lefties in your life on the road to beautiful handwriting.

You dumped all
I have mentioned in the Past
that text doest work that I have
a low reading comprehention and I thought you
would have remebered somthing like that, I'm I'm the kind of Person when
that is Passive. I'm the kind of Person when
Someone brings up a Problem I wanted to fix it then and
you saying "I'm going to bed soon" said that he arnt going to fix it
that night
I was annoyed because

and always remember... LEFTIES ROCK!

Manufactured by Amazon.ca
Bolton, ON